AMAZE
BALLS

AMAZE-BALLS

An Hachette UK Company
www.hachette.co.uk

Summersdale Publishers Ltd
Part of Octopus Publishing Group Limited
Carmelite House
50 Victoria Embankment
LONDON
EC4Y 0DZ
UK

www.summersdale.com

Printed and bound in China

ISBN: 978-1-78783-025-7

Substantial discounts on bulk quantities of Summersdale books are available to corporations, professional associations and other organisations. For details contact general enquiries: telephone: +44 (0) 1243 771107 or email: enquiries@summersdale.com.

AMAZE
BALLS

SWEET AND SAVOURY RECIPES FOR THE
ULTIMATE BITE-SIZED SNACKS

summersdale

CONTENTS

INTRODUCTION

There is something inexplicable and deeply satisfying about eating bite-sized food, and creating it is great fun too!

The first chapter in this book is dedicated to healthy energy balls. These are the most super of superfoods and are *all* nutritious, delicious snacks for any time of day. From a grab-and-go breakfast or a post-gym protein boost, to a vitamin-loaded lunch box treat or an antioxidant immunity boost, these recipes are bursting with highly nutritional ingredients such as matcha green tea, cacao powder, flax and chia seeds, and spirulina. Many recipes are vegan and many don't need baking.

The second chapter features savoury balls. Some are mini versions of classics, including garlic dough balls and Scotch eggs, and others are inspired by world street food. Most are vegetarian and all are ideal picnic and party foods.

Saving the 'naughty-but-nice' chapter till last, we have the sweet balls. These are definitely on the treat list, and include mini jam doughnuts and cute cake pops. These are great for parties and will guarantee your popularity as the host with the most!

So, without further ado, let's go amaze-balls mad!

NOTE ON INGREDIENTS

All of the ingredients listed in the recipes should be available in your local health-food store or larger supermarket.

Many of the energy ball recipes include dates as they create a perfect sticky consistency to bind the other ingredients together. Medjool dates are large, soft, dark and juicy with a caramel flavour. However, they are quite pricy, so ordinary soft pitted dates have been used in many of the recipes instead.

Another key ingredient in energy balls is nut butter – you can pretty much turn any nut or seed into butter, and there are so many to choose from on the market. If you prefer, you can substitute your favourite for those stated in the recipes.

Although oats are naturally gluten-free (oats contain avenin, which is a protein similar to gluten), they can become contaminated by other grains during processing, so buy gluten-free oats if you want to be sure.

To adapt recipes containing flour so that they become gluten free, substitute one of the huge range of gluten-free flours available. As they all have different characteristics, you will need to look up the substitution quantity, and you may also need to add xanthan gum to help doughs and batters rise.

To make any vegetarian energy ball vegan, swap the non-vegan ingredient for an alternative; for example, use agave nectar instead of honey.

For recipes included in the Savoury and Sweet chapters you may wish to experiment with vegan-friendly alternatives too. Vegan butter, cheese and milk substitutes are becoming widely available – just check the label to make sure it can be heated if required by the recipe. There are also a few vegan egg products on the market that focus on replicating the binding, leavening and thickening properties of eggs.

CONVERSIONS AND MEASUREMENTS

All the conversions in the tables below are close approximates, which have been rounded up or down. When following a recipe, always stick to one unit of measurement and do not alternate between them.

Imperial		Metric
½ oz	(≈)	10 g
¾ oz	(≈)	20 g
1 oz	(≈)	25 g
1½ oz	(≈)	40 g
2 oz	(≈)	50 g
2½ oz	(≈)	60 g
3 oz	(≈)	75 g
4 oz	(≈)	110 g
4½ oz	(≈)	125 g
5 oz	(≈)	150 g
6 oz	(≈)	175 g
7 oz	(≈)	200 g
8 oz	(≈)	225 g
9 oz	(≈)	250 g
10 oz	(≈)	275 g
12 oz	(≈)	350 g
1 lb	(≈)	450 g

Liquid measurements
6 ml = 1 tsp
15 ml = 1 tbsp
30 ml = ⅛ cup
60 ml = ¼ cup
120 ml = ½ cup
240 ml = 1 cup

Butter measurements
30 g = ⅛ cup
55 g = ¼ cup
75 g = ⅓ cup
110 g = ½ cup
150 g = ⅔ cup
170 g = ¾ cup
225 g = 1 cup

Dried ingredient measurements
5 g = 1 tsp
15 g = 1 tbsp
150 g flour = 1 cup
225 g caster sugar = 1 cup
115 g icing sugar = 1 cup
175 g brown sugar = 1 cup
200 g sprinkles = 1 cup

HANDY HINTS ON MAKING THE PERFECT AMAZE-BALLS

- If the mixture feels a bit too sticky, chill it for 15 minutes or so in the fridge or freezer.

- If the mixture seems too moist, add a dry ingredient, for example rolled oats, ground almonds or coconut flour.

- If the mixture seems too dry, add liquid in the form of agave nectar, honey or a nut butter.

- Wet your hands to stop the mixture from sticking to them when balling.

DIETARY REQUIREMENTS

Look for the following symbols to find out whether a recipe is suitable for vegetarians or vegans, and whether it requires cooking or not:

 Vegetarian

 Vegan

 Cooking required

 No cooking required

ENERGY BALLS

Pistachio and Cranberry Crunch • Matcha
and Cacao Buzz Balls • Apricot and Coconut
Lunch Box Balls • Chewy Chocolate and
Chia • Nutty Pumpkin and Coconut •
Spicy Pecan Balls • Bountiful Coconut and
Chocolate Energy Balls • 'Granola to Go' •
Cranberry and Sunflower Seed • Brownie
Balls • Crunchy Chocolate Chip • Cherry
and Coconut • Maple and Pumpkin Pie •
Carrot Cake • Very Berry Balls • Matcha
and Nut Blast • Terrific Almond Truffles •
Apple Crumble Balls • Chocolate Cherry
Picnic • Zesty Lemon and Coconut •
Pistachio and Yoghurt • Beetroot Beauties •
Peanut Butter and Cacao Superballs •
Zingy Sweet Potato and Ginger • Chia and
Cherry Surprise • Pina Colada Balls •
Spirulina, Date and Mint • Chocolate,
Avocado and Coconut • Decadent Quinoa
and Chocolate • Sea Buckthorn Balls

PISTACHIO AND CRANBERRY CRUNCH

As tasty as they are beautiful! Emerald-coloured pistachios and ruby-red cranberries are the perfect combination, making a deliciously healthy jewel of a treat.

Method

Blitz the pistachios in a food processor until chopped and place to one side.

Repeat with the cranberries and put aside with the pistachios.

Pulse the dates, agave nectar, ground chia seeds and salt in the food processor until the mixture starts to form a sticky dough then add in the already chopped pistachios and cranberries.

Refrigerate for 30 minutes before balling.

These little jewels will keep in an airtight container in the fridge for up to a week.

Makes

Approximately 14 balls

Ingredients

100 g pistachios
100 g dried cranberries
200 g dates
2 tbsp agave nectar
1 tbsp ground
   chia seeds
pinch of sea salt

Did you know?
Matcha, unlike other green teas, is grown in shade and not dried or heated. The whole leaf is stoneground to help preserve its nutrients. It is high in antioxidants, containing over 130 more than regular green tea.

MATCHA AND CACAO BUZZ BALLS

Glorious balls combining the luxury of dates and the richness of chocolate with a superfood blast of matcha to keep you buzzing with energy. Gluten free too!

Method

Blitz the dates and raisins in a food processor until they form a nice sticky paste.

Sprinkle in the cacao, matcha powder and almonds and pulse till combined.

Add 1 teaspoon of agave nectar and combine; if the mixture won't form into a ball, add the other teaspoon.

Scoop a small tablespoon of mixture into the palm of your hand and roll it into a ball. Repeat until you have used up all of the mixture.

Place on a tray, sprinkle with extra matcha powder then chill for about an hour before sealing in an airtight container.

Store (or hide!) in the fridge for up to 2 weeks (although it's highly unlikely they will stick around that long!).

Makes

Approximately 12 balls

Ingredients

150 g medjool dates
50 g raisins
4 tbsp raw cacao powder
1 tbsp matcha green tea powder (plus some for dusting)
50 g ground almonds
1–2 tsp agave nectar

Did you know?
Coconut oil is said to boost good cholesterol levels in the body and to help fight infection.

APRICOT AND COCONUT LUNCH BOX BALLS

Sweet and nutty: the kids will be begging to have these little 'super snacks' in their lunch boxes every day – just don't let on how healthy they are. Super-quick to make too!

Method

Pop all the ingredients into a food processor and blitz until the mixture is combined (if the mixture seems dry you can add a few drops of water or coconut oil and reblitz).

Scoop a small tablespoon of the mixture into the palm of your hand and squeeze into a ball. Repeat until you have used up all of the mixture.

Gently roll the balls in the extra desiccated coconut to coat.

Then pop them on a tray in the fridge to chill for an hour before sealing them in an airtight container.

They will last for up to 2 weeks in the fridge.

Makes

Approximately
16–18 balls

Ingredients

200 g dried apricots

75 g desiccated coconut (plus some for coating)

50 g ground almonds

1 tbsp coconut oil

2 tbsp honey

2–3 drops of vanilla extract

CHEWY CHOCOLATE AND CHIA

Deliciously chocolatey and fudgy, these will become a favourite in both gym bag and school bag, keeping everyone energised all day long.

Method

Pop the pistachios in a food processor and whizz until very finely chopped – empty out and set aside for coating.

Blitz the dates into a paste, then add the remaining ingredients and pulse until combined.

Let the mixture chill in the fridge for 15 minutes.

Roll a bite-sized piece of the refrigerated mixture between the palms of your hands. Repeat until you have used up all of the mixture.

Roll half of the balls in the white chocolate flakes or shredded coconut and the other half in the ground pistachios.

Keep in the fridge in an airtight container for up to a week.

Makes

Approximately 14 balls

Ingredients

For the balls:
200 g medjool dates
50 g rolled oats
3 tbsp raw
    cacao powder
1 tbsp chia seeds
1 tbsp agave nectar
½ tsp sea salt
Seeds from
    1 vanilla pod

For the coating:
75 g crushed pistachios
75 g white chocolate
    flakes or shredded
    coconut

Did you know?
Butternut squash seeds can be lightly roasted in the oven and eaten as a healthy alternative to salty snacks.

NUTTY PUMPKIN AND COCONUT

Perfect for Halloween, these gorgeous pumpkin balls are a naturally sweet treat. There won't be any tricks with these on hand!

Method

Prepare the pumpkin or butternut squash by cutting off the top and bottom and peeling with a vegetable peeler. Cut in half and remove the seeds and fibrous membrane. Cut into 3-cm (1¼-in.) cubes and steam for 20 minutes until soft.

Blitz the pecans in a food processor until they are finely chopped. Add in all the other ingredients and pulse until the mixture is combined and smooth. Chill the mixture if needed to make it easier to roll.

Spoon out enough mixture to create a 3-cm (1¼-in.) ball, roll into a ball in your hands, and then roll lightly in the desiccated coconut.

Arrange the balls on a tray lined with non-stick parchment and put them back in the fridge to fully set before transferring them to an airtight container.

These will keep in the fridge for up to 5 days.

Makes

Approximately 14 balls

Ingredients

For the balls:
225 g pumpkin or butternut squash
75 g pecans
2 tbsp smooth almond butter
75 g rolled oats
2 tbsp honey
½ tsp cinnamon ground
pinch of sea salt

For the coating:
desiccated coconut

SPICY PECAN BALLS

Deliciously warming spices and pecans make this gluten-free, vegan ball of energy very moreish. You'll want to make them all the time!

Method

Whizz the dates and apricots together in a food processor until they come together as a sticky ball.

Add the pecans and carrots and whizz again until smooth.

Add the coconut flour, almonds and spices and keep blitzing until smooth and combined.

Pop in the fridge for 15 minutes before rolling into balls.

These will keep in an airtight container in the fridge for up to 4 days.

Makes

Approximately 12 balls

Ingredients

150 g dates

50 g dried apricots

50 g pecans

25 g finely
   grated carrot

10 g coconut flour

10 g ground almonds

½ tsp ground
   cinnamon

¼ tsp ground cloves

¼ tsp ground
   star anise

Did you know?
Raw cacao powder is made by cold-pressing unroasted cacao beans. This process retains the living enzymes and removes the fat (cacao butter). Cocoa powder is created after the beans are finely ground into a powder and roasted at high temperatures.

BOUNTIFUL COCONUT AND CHOCOLATE ENERGY BALLS

These wonderfully rich energy balls have a truly tropical taste – if you can resist eating them all in one go they will last in the fridge in an airtight container for up to a month.

Method

Mix the dry ingredients (including the chocolate) in a bowl and combine thoroughly.

In a heatproof bowl melt the coconut oil and honey, either in the microwave for 10–20 seconds or by using a bain-marie, and stir frequently. Pour the dry ingredients mix into the wet, adding the vanilla extract, and bind them together to form a dough. In a separate small bowl mix the cacao powder and icing sugar.

Make 3-cm (1¼-in.) round balls by spooning a tablespoon of the mixture into the palm of your hand and rolling it to make a ball – speed is of the essence here as the coconut oil can get rather sticky.

Place the balls in the sugar and cacao mix, rolling them about until fully coated, then rest each one on a cool plate. Place in the freezer to harden, for up to an hour.

Makes

Approximately 25 balls

Ingredients

For the balls:
125 g ground almonds
50 g coconut flour
75 g rolled oats
100 g dark chocolate, blitzed in a food processor
pinch of sea salt
3 tbsp coconut oil
3 tbsp honey
1 tsp vanilla extract

To coat the balls:
2 tbsp cacao powder
2 tsp icing sugar

'GRANOLA TO GO'

Packed full of nutty crunch and the satisfying sweetness of honey and banana, these balls are perfect for breakfast on the go.

Method

Place all the ingredients into a food processor and blitz until fully combined (you may need to scrape gooey bits off the base of the bowl every so often).

If needed, pop in the fridge for 15 minutes to firm up.

Squeeze each portion of mixture in your hands before rolling into a ball.

These will keep refrigerated in a sealed container for 5 days.

Makes

Approximately 12 balls

Ingredients

150 g medjool dates

75 g granola

20 g walnut pieces

20 g dried
   banana chips

2 tbsp raw
   cacao powder

2 tbsp almond butter

2 tbsp honey

Did you know?
Flaxseeds were grown by ancient civilisations. They provide one of the best sources of omega-3 fatty acids. Use either brown or golden, and if you prefer less crunch buy them milled.

CRANBERRY AND SUNFLOWER SEED

These are bursting with superfood chia and flaxseeds, packed full of protein and healthy fats from the almonds and nut butter and offer a vitamin hit from the cranberries.

Method

Blitz the dates to a paste in a food processor.

Lightly toast the oats and almonds in a non-stick frying pan (no oil needed) for a few minutes on medium heat until they smell toasty. Pop them into the food processor with the dates.

Add all remaining ingredients and pulse until combined.

Refrigerate the mixture for 30 minutes and then roll it into 3-cm (1¼-in.) balls.

Keep in the fridge in an airtight container for up to a week.

Makes

Approximately 12 balls

Ingredients

150 g dates
75 g rolled oats
75 g almonds,
    finely chopped
3 tbsp almond butter
2 tbsp honey
1 tbsp coconut oil
1 tbsp ground flaxseeds
1 tbsp chia seeds
1 tbsp sunflower seeds
1 tsp almond extract
75 g dried cranberries

BROWNIE BALLS

It's hard to believe these are actually a healthy snack as they are so chocolatey and chewy. Yet thanks to the cacao and dark chocolate they are bursting with antioxidants and minerals.

Method

Blitz the dates and raisins in a food processor until you have a sticky ball.

Add the remaining ingredients and continue to pulse until combined.

If the mixture is a little dry, add 1 or 2 teaspoons of agave nectar or honey.

Roll into 3-cm (1¼-in.) balls then roll each ball in the desiccated coconut, or grated dark chocolate if you prefer, before placing in the fridge in an airtight container.

These will keep in the fridge for a week or can be frozen for up to 3 months. Don't be surprised though if they've all been enjoyed in just a couple of days!

Makes

Approximately 12 balls

Ingredients

For the balls:
150 g medjool dates
50 g golden raisins
50 g ground almonds
3 tbsp raw
   cacao powder
50 g grated dark
   chocolate
1 tbsp coconut oil
pinch of sea salt
1–2 tsp agave nectar
   or honey (optional)

For the coating:
desiccated coconut
   or finely grated
   dark chocolate

CRUNCHY CHOCOLATE CHIP

Bursting with protein, vitamins and minerals, as well as good fats and fibre, these balls are perfect to fill you up and keep you going till lunchtime.

Method

Pop the banana and cashew butter in a food processor and blitz until smooth.

Add the oats, flaxseeds, honey and sea salt, and pulse until just combined.

Stir in the chocolate chips by hand.

Let the mixture chill in the fridge for at least 30 minutes then form into balls.

Best stored in the freezer in an airtight container until ready to eat, as they contain fresh banana. They defrost very quickly so you'll only need to wait 15 minutes.

Makes

Approximately 12 balls

Ingredients

1 large overripe
   banana
2 tbsp cashew butter
180 g rolled oats
1 tbsp ground flaxseeds
1 tbsp honey
pinch of sea salt
3 tbsp chocolate chips
   (dark or milk,
   as you like it)

CHERRY AND COCONUT

Yummy chewy tart cherry balls are so moreish you'll need to make more than required, as once you take a bite, you might accidentally eat the lot.

Method

Blitz the dates and tart cherries in a food processor until they form a smooth paste.

Add the pitted cherries and pulse until combined.

Add the remaining ingredients and process on high speed until you've created a dough.

If needed, place in the fridge for about 30 minutes to firm up before rolling into balls.

Coat them by rolling in the desiccated coconut.

Store in an airtight container in the fridge for up to 5 days or you can freeze them for up to 3 months.

Makes

Approximately 14 balls

Ingredients

For the balls:
150 g dates
50 g dried tart cherries
50 g pitted cherries
1 tbsp freeze-dried cherry powder (optional)
50 g shredded coconut
50 g rolled oats
½ tsp vanilla extract

For the coating:
desiccated coconut

Did you know?
It takes about 40 litres of sap to make 1 litre of maple syrup.

MAPLE AND PUMPKIN PIE

Such a delicious flavour combination of maple syrup, pumpkin and pecans. Keep them on hand as an afternoon energy treat.

Method

To prepare the pumpkin or butternut squash, cut off the top and bottom and peel with a vegetable peeler. Cut in half and remove the seeds and fibrous membrane. Cut into 3-cm (1¼-in.) cubes and steam for 20 minutes until soft.

Toast the oats and pecans in a non-stick frying pan until they are lightly coloured and have a nutty aroma.

Blitz the dates in a food processor until they form a sticky ball.

Add the maple syrup, pumpkin, chia seeds, cinnamon and salt and pulse until combined.

Add the oats and pecans and pulse again.

If needed, chill the mixture in the fridge for 30 minutes before rolling into balls.

These will keep in an airtight container in the fridge for a week or you can freeze them for up to 3 months.

Makes

Approximately 12 balls

Ingredients

100 g pumpkin or
    butternut squash
75 g rolled oats
50 g pecans,
    roughly chopped
100 g dates
1 tbsp maple syrup
1 tbsp chia seeds
½ tsp cinnamon
pinch of sea salt

Did you know?
The addition of
protein powder gives
these an added
energy boost.

CARROT CAKE

Good news! You can have your cake and eat it! A guilt-free way to enjoy your favourite carrot cake flavours. So simple to make too!

Method

Simply pop all the ingredients in a food processor and blitz until fully combined.

If necessary, chill the mixture in the fridge for 15 minutes before balling.

Once you have a tray of bite-sized balls roll them in the cinnamon and desiccated coconut and store in an airtight container in the fridge for up to 5 days.

Makes

Approximately 12 balls

Ingredients

For the balls:
50 g rolled oats
50 g ground almonds
100 g dried apricots
25 g walnuts
2 tbsp almond butter
1 tbsp vanilla plant-based protein powder
50 g grated carrot
½ tsp ground cinnamon
1 tsp vanilla extract
zest of 1 orange
pinch of grated nutmeg

For the coating:
desiccated coconut
pinch of ground cinnamon

VERY BERRY BALLS

Enjoy a walk in the early autumn sunshine and forage in the hedgerows for some juicy blackberries to make these raw blackberry energy balls.

Method

Whizz the dates and raisins together in a food processor until they form a sticky paste.

Add the remaining ingredients and pulse until combined.

Place in the freezer for 15 minutes to firm up the mixture.

Take tablespoon-sized pieces and roll them into balls.

These are best stored in the freezer in a sealed container for up to 3 months.

Makes

Approximately 12 balls

Ingredients

100 g dates
70 g raisins
100 g blackberries
2 tbsp freeze-dried
    blackberry powder
150 g ground almonds
1 tsp vanilla pod seeds

MATCHA AND NUT BLAST

These matcha and nut energy balls are loaded with superfood goodness to keep you energised morning, noon and night.

Method

Place the dates, maple syrup, matcha powder and salt in a food processor and blitz until they form a paste.

Transfer the date paste to a mixing bowl, adding the coconut and chopped nuts and stirring really well to combine.

Chill the mixture in the fridge for at least 30 minutes before rolling into bite-sized balls. Keep your hands dampened with water as this process can get a bit sticky!

Store in the fridge in an airtight container for up to a week.

Makes

Approximately 14 balls

Ingredients

200 g medjool dates
2 tbsp maple syrup
3 tbsp matcha powder
pinch of sea salt
20 g coconut, shredded
25 g cashews,
    finely chopped
75 g pistachios,
    finely chopped

TERRIFIC ALMOND TRUFFLES

Try out these indulgent and fabulously fudgy almond truffles. Have fun experimenting with the flavouring with coffee, orange or peppermint extract. You could even create an after-dinner petit four lucky dip!

Method

Pop all the ingredients into a food processor and blitz until they form a sticky dough.

Take a small tablespoon of mixture and roll it between your palms to form a ball, then roll it in the cocoa and cacao powder mixture.

Store in the fridge in an airtight container.

They will last for 2 weeks, but I'd be VERY surprised if they hang around that long!

Makes

Approximately 12 balls

Ingredients

For the balls:
200 g medjool dates
50 g ground almonds
4 tbsp raw
    cacao powder
1 tbsp coconut oil
1 tbsp agave nectar
1 tsp almond extract,
    or other flavouring
    of your choice
½ tsp sea salt

For the coating:
sweetened cocoa
    powder
raw cacao powder

APPLE CRUMBLE BALLS

No, they don't come with custard. However, with the delicious combination of apple, nuts and oats you won't miss it.

Method

Make the apple puree in advance so it has time to cool – peel, core and slice your choice of apples and microwave on high power for 3 minutes before mashing them.

Pop all the remaining ingredients into a food processor and blitz until combined.

Chill in the fridge for about 30 minutes to firm up before rolling into balls.

Because of the raw apple these will only keep for 4 days in the fridge, but they are so tasty they will be long gone by then. Or you can keep them in the freezer for up to 3 months. They thaw quickly in around 15 minutes.

Makes

Approximately 16 balls

Ingredients

150 g apple puree
— make your own
with 2 apples, or
buy unsweetened
20 g grated apple
100 g raisins
2 tbsp almond butter
100 g rolled oats
50 g pecans

CHOCOLATE CHERRY PICNIC

So delicious... cherries and chocolate: these no-bake healthy snacks are positively popping with flavour. Luckily they are so simple to make that you won't struggle to keep up with demand!

Method

Pop all the ingredients into a food processor and blitz until combined.

Chill the mixture in the fridge for about 30 minutes to firm up before rolling into balls.

The balls will keep in the fridge in an airtight container for up to a week.

Makes

10–12 balls

Ingredients

100 g rolled oats

50 g dark chocolate chips

50 g dried cherries

50 g dried cranberries

1 tbsp milled chia seeds

2 tbsp almond butter

2 tbsp agave nectar

1 tbsp coconut oil

ZESTY LEMON AND COCONUT

The lemon juice and zest give these energy balls a refreshing clean taste and would be a welcome healthy dessert alternative.

Method

Blitz the cashews in a food processor at high speed until they resemble breadcrumbs.

Add in the remaining ingredients and pulse until the mixture comes together into a smooth dough.

Roll into 3-cm (1¼-in.) balls and continue until all the mixture is used. Then roll them in the unsweetened shredded coconut before popping them in the fridge to chill for 30 minutes before eating.

Keep them in an airtight container in the fridge for up to a week.

Makes

Approximately 12 balls

Ingredients

For the balls:
100 g cashews
50 g coconut flour
35 g coconut, unsweetened, shredded
45 ml lemon juice
2 tbsp honey
1 tbsp coconut oil
zest of 1 lemon

For the coating:
unsweetened shredded coconut

Did you know?
Pistachios are very high in antioxidants, especially lutein which is essential for healthy eyes. Eating a handful of pistachios will give you more potassium than eating a banana.

PISTACHIO AND YOGHURT

Packed full of antioxidants and potassium from the pistachios, these will provide a great post-workout reward.

Method

Pop the pistachios into a food processor and blitz until finely chopped.

Add the dates and process again until they form a sticky dough.

Add the maple syrup and give the mixture one final whizz before rolling into balls.

Chill in the fridge while you make the topping.

For the topping, beat together the yoghurt and cream cheese before beating in the icing sugar.

Once the balls are chilled, dunk them halfway into the topping mixture before finishing off with a light dusting of freeze-dried fruit powder (optional).

These will keep in a sealed container in the fridge for up to 5 days.

Makes

Approximately 12 balls

Ingredients

For the balls:
100 g pistachios
200 g dates
1 tbsp maple syrup

For the topping:
2 tbsp plain or
  vanilla yoghurt
2 tbsp cream cheese
4 tbsp icing sugar,
  sieved
freeze-dried raspberry/
  strawberry powder
  (optional)

BEETROOT BEAUTIES

Not only is beetroot a great detoxifier, it packs these balls with fibre, folate, vitamin C and antioxidants. If that's not enough... they're also pretty and pink!

Method

Blitz the dates into a sticky ball.

Add in the cashew nut butter and pulse until smooth.

Add all remaining ingredients and pulse until combined.

If the mixture seems too wet, add a few more oats before rolling into balls.

These are best stored in the freezer in an airtight container for up to 3 months.

Makes

Approximately 12 balls

Ingredients

For the balls:
100 g dates
2 tbsp cashew
    nut butter
100 g cooked beetroot
1 tbsp freeze-dried
    beetroot powder
    (optional)
3 tbsp chocolate
    protein powder
20 g ground almonds
120 g rolled oats

For the coating:
desiccated coconut

Did you know?
If you want to keep these balls vegan then opt for plant-based protein powder — there are lots to choose from, and they are often a blend of pea, hemp seed, soya and pumpkin seed proteins.

PEANUT BUTTER AND CACAO SUPERBALLS

Pop these in your gym bag as they are perfect for a post-workout protein boost, and great for muscle repair.

Method

In a mixing bowl measure out the peanut butter, agave nectar and vanilla.

Stir until these ingredients are combined and then add in the protein powder and cacao powder.

Once the mixture is smooth you can start to shape it into balls. If you find the mixture gets a bit on the sticky side, add a smidge more protein powder.

Pop them in the fridge in an airtight container and they will keep for 7 days.

Makes

Approximately 12 balls

Ingredients

4 tbsp peanut butter
    (smooth or crunchy)
2 tbsp agave nectar
½ tsp vanilla extract
25 g chocolate
    protein powder
20 g raw cacao powder

Did you know?
Ginger has a very long history of use in various forms of traditional and alternative medicine. It is used to help digestion, reduce nausea, help fight the flu and common cold, and as an anti-inflammatory to relieve muscle and joint pain.
The list goes on!

ZINGY SWEET POTATO AND GINGER

These combine the satisfying taste of sweet potato with a zingy afterburner from the ginger. Great for any time of day but also as a perfectly balanced pre-exercise snack as they're full of slow-release carbs mixed with good fats and protein, and a source of potassium, manganese, and vitamins A, B6 and C.

Method

To cook the sweet potato: peel and cut into even-sized pieces and then steam for about 20 minutes until soft. Allow to cool before chilling in the fridge for an hour until completely cold.

Blitz the sweet potato in a food processor.

Pop in all the other ingredients and pulse until thoroughly combined.

Leave the mixture to chill in the fridge for about 30 minutes.

Break off bite-sized pieces of the dough, roll them into balls and then coat them with the shredded coconut.

Store them in the fridge for up to 5 days in a sealed container.

Makes

Approximately 14 balls

Ingredients

For the balls:
200 g sweet potato (1 medium-sized)
100 g rolled oats
2 tbsp almond butter
1 tbsp honey
2 tsp ginger puree (you can double this if ginger is your thing!)
½ tsp ground nutmeg
¼ tsp ground cinnamon (optional)

For the coating:
shredded coconut

Did you know?
Chia seeds are native to southern Mexico and known as 'the running food'. When mixed with water they provide a high-energy and nutrient-rich drink.

CHIA AND CHERRY SURPRISE

What a surprise to discover a whole juicy cherry in the middle when you take your first bite. Head out for a ramble armed with some in your day pack to give you a superfood boost.

Method

Whizz the dates in the food processor to a sticky paste.

Add the other ingredients, except the cherries, and mix well until fully combined.

Chill in the fridge for 15 minutes to firm up.

Take a small tablespoon of mixture and create a pocket for the cherry. Place a cherry into the pocket, then close the mixture around it and roll it into a ball before coating with poppy seeds.

These will keep in a sealed container in the fridge for up to 5 days.

Makes

12–14 balls

Ingredients

200 g medjool dates
2 tbsp chia seeds
2 tbsp poppy seeds
   (plus extra
   for coating)
2 tbsp raw
   cacao powder
2 tbsp cashew
   nut butter
12–14 fresh
   cherries, pitted

PINA COLADA BALLS

These pina colada flavours will transport you to a tropical white sandy beach with the sound of waves lapping on the shore – well, perhaps that's a slight exaggeration! However, they are totally delicious, and the cashews make them high in iron and soluble dietary fibre.

Method

Pop the cashews in a food processor and blitz until very finely chopped.

Add all the remaining ingredients and process until the mixture forms a dough.

Put the dough in the fridge to chill for about 15 minutes.

Take large teaspoons of the dough and roll into balls before coating them in the desiccated coconut.

Store in an airtight container in the fridge for up to a week.

Makes

18–20 balls

Ingredients

For the balls:
100 g cashews
50 g coconut flour
35 g unsweetened
    shredded coconut
45 ml pineapple juice
2 tbsp agave nectar
1 tbsp coconut oil

For the coating:
desiccated coconut

SPIRULINA, DATE AND MINT

'May contain algae' – perhaps keep this info to yourself until the kids have tried them! Spirulina truly is the ultimate superfood – it contains all nine essential amino acids and is loaded with calcium, iron, magnesium, and vitamins A, E and K.

Method

Add the cashews, oats, spirulina and mint to a food processor and blitz until finely chopped and fully combined.

Add the dates and nut butter and process again until the mixture forms a dough.

Roll into balls and then pop into an airtight container and store in the fridge for up to a week.

Makes

Approximately 12 balls

Ingredients

100 g cashew nuts
50 g rolled oats
1 tbsp spirulina
½ tsp dried mint or
    4 fresh leaves
200 g medjool dates
2 tbsp raw cashew
    or almond butter

CHOCOLATE, AVOCADO AND COCONUT

It is probably easier to list which nutrients aren't in an avocado – they contain over 20 vitamins and minerals, antioxidants, good fats and soluble fibre. With all these nutritious and delicious ingredients your body – and your taste buds – will love you for eating these balls.

Method

Pop all ingredients in the food processor and pulse until fully combined.

The ripeness and size of your avocado will determine the stiffness of the mixture. If it seems too stiff add a little more agave nectar.

Take small tablespoons of the mixture and roll them into balls then coat them in the coconut.

Pop them on a tray in the fridge to chill for about 30 minutes before transferring them to a sealed container. These will only keep for a couple of days, so gobble them up quick!

Makes

10–12 balls

Ingredients

For the balls:
flesh of 1 large,
    ripe avocado
2 tbsp almond butter
150 g rolled oats
3 tbsp raw
    cacao powder
1 tsp vanilla extract
1 tbsp agave nectar

For the coating:
desiccated coconut

Did you know?
Quinoa is a complete protein, containing all nine essential amino acids: great for those following a vegan or vegetarian diet.

DECADENT QUINOA AND CHOCOLATE

So decadent you'll need to remind yourself they're healthy energy-boosting balls.

Method

Cook the white quinoa as per the packet instructions, then set aside to cool for 15 minutes before chilling in the fridge until completely cold.

Blitz the raisins in a food processor until they become a sticky paste.

Add the oats, nut butter, cacao, quinoa and honey and keep pulsing until you have a fully blended dough. Lastly, add the chocolate chips and pulse a couple of times to blend.

Leave to chill in the fridge for around 30 minutes.

To turn the dough into irresistible bite-sized balls, take a small tablespoon of the mixture and roll it between your palms – if this is a bit sticky just dampen your hands with water. Repeat until you have used up all of the mixture.

Pop the finished balls in an airtight container and store in the fridge for up to a week.

Makes

Approximately 14 balls

Ingredients

50 g white quinoa, washed

200 g raisins

50 g rolled oats

2 tbsp almond butter, softened

2 tbsp raw cacao powder

2 tbsp honey

2 tbsp dark chocolate chips

Did you know?
Sea buckthorn berries
are unrivalled in the plant
kingdom for their high
content of vitamins
A, E and K.

SEA BUCKTHORN BALLS

Sea buckthorn berries have a strong citrus-like aroma and contain concentrated levels of vitamins, including more vitamin C than any other fruit. They also contain antioxidants and good fats. You can choose your favourite nuts to go in the energy balls, but macadamia, cashews and almonds all work well.

Method

Blitz the dates, raisins and sea buckthorn berries in the food processor to form a paste.

Add in the remaining ingredients and pulse until combined.

Chill in the fridge for 15 minutes and then you can get balling.

Pop them in an airtight container and store in the fridge for up to a week.

Makes

Approximately 12 balls

Ingredients

100 g medjool dates

50 g raisins

50 g sea buckthorn berries

100 g mixed nuts of your choice

1 tbsp milled chia seeds

2 tbsp almond butter

2 tbsp agave nectar

OTHER AMAZE-BALLS
SAVOURY

Falafel and Tahini • Chickpea, Carrot and Corn • Moringa Flower Fritters • Baked Cheesy Olives • Scotch Quail Eggs • French Gougères • Cranberry and Goat Cheese • Japanese Rice Balls • Buttery Potato Dumplings • Sev Puri Puffs • Cheesy Potato Balls • Mac and Cheese Balls • Garlic Dough Balls • Cheese and Mushroom Arancini

FALAFEL AND TAHINI

This dish is easy to make, packed with fresh herbs and flavour, and by swapping normal flour for chickpea flour you can make it gluten free. It's also naturally vegan.

Method

To make the falafels:

Drain the chickpeas and dry them before popping all the ingredients into a food processor. Blitz until the mixture is smooth. Roll the mixture into balls.

Pour enough sunflower oil into a deep pan to cover the base, and heat until it sizzles. Add the balls and shallow-fry, turning regularly, until evenly golden. Serve with the tahini sauce. Most delicious served warm but will keep in the fridge for up to 5 days.

To make the tahini sauce:

Whisk together the crushed garlic and tahini paste. Gradually whisk in the lemon juice until the mixture lightens and thickens. If it is too thick you can add a little water. Pop the sauce in the fridge until you're ready to serve and then drizzle with olive oil, if you like, and sprinkle with the chopped flat-leaf parsley.

Makes

Approximately 16 balls

Ingredients

For the falafels:
400 g can chickpeas
2 garlic cloves, chopped
1 tbsp harissa
2 tsp ground cumin
2 tsp ground coriander
2 tbsp chickpea flour
zest of 1 lemon
1 handful of coriander
sunflower oil, for frying

For the tahini sauce:
4 garlic cloves, crushed
3 tbsp tahini paste
juice of 2 lemons
1 tbsp olive oil (optional)
1 tbsp chopped flat-leaf parsley

CHICKPEA, CARROT AND CORN

Keep plenty on hand in the summer for picnics and parties. Delicious when dipped in a spicy harissa sauce and perfect for adding some oomph to salads.

Method

Pop all the ingredients except the sweetcorn and peas – add these later for a bit of texture – in a food processor and pulse until combined. Don't over process it as you still want to keep some texture.

Add the sweetcorn and peas and stir to combine.

Chill the mixture for 20 minutes.

Take bite-sized pieces of mixture and roll them into balls, shallow-frying in sizzling oil until golden.

Drain and serve on the same day as a hot or cold snack. The uncooked mixture lasts for about 3 days in an airtight container in the fridge.

Makes

Approximately 12 balls

Ingredients

400 g can chickpeas, drained
50 g finely grated carrot
    (moisture squeezed out)
1 red chilli, finely chopped
1 tbsp fresh coriander,
    chopped
1 garlic clove, crushed
1 tsp cumin seeds
1 tsp dried coriander
1 tbsp baking powder
1 tbsp chickpea flour
2 tbsp chopped fresh parsley
zest of 1 lemon
pinch of sea salt
ground black pepper
50 g sweetcorn
50 g peas
sunflower oil, for frying

Did you know?
Moringa trees are referred
to in their native India as
the 'Tree of Life'.

MORINGA FLOWER FRITTERS

The bark, root, stems, seed pods, leaves and flowers of the Moringa tree are all used for culinary, medicinal or practical purposes. Hailed as a superfood, the leaves have seven times the amount of vitamin C as an orange, four times the calcium of milk and four times the beta-carotene of carrots.

Method

Make a paste of the chilli and garlic – using a pestle and mortar if you have one.

Place the flour, salt and turmeric in a mixing bowl with the flowers, leaves, garlic and chilli paste, and mix together well.

Add enough water while mixing to create a thick batter and mould it into balls.

Heat the vegetable oil in a pan and carefully lower the balls a few at a time into the oil and fry, turning until evenly golden.

Drain and serve.

Makes

Approximately 6 balls

Ingredients

2 green chillies, deseeded and chopped
6 garlic cloves, peeled
150 g chickpea flour
1 tsp sea salt
1 tsp turmeric
1 cup moringa flowers, washed and chopped
2 tbsp moringa leaves, washed and chopped
water
vegetable oil for frying

BAKED CHEESY OLIVES

You'll want to dust off the Martini glasses to accompany these retro canapés. Don't pre-judge this one! Prepare to be pleasantly surprised by how wonderfully these cheesy, salty flavours combine into the perfect party nibble.

Method

Drain the olives and dry on kitchen paper.

Pop the flour, cheeses, butter and spices in a food processor and pulse on low until the mixture comes together to form a dough (if it is too dry add a teaspoon or two of water until a dough forms).

Take a small piece of dough and flatten into a 5-cm (2-in.) circle in the palm of your hand. Put an olive in the middle and bring the dough around the olive until it is covered then roll into a ball, fully sealing the edges.

Allow the balls to chill in the fridge for an hour.

Bake the olives in a preheated oven at 200°C/400°F/Gas 6 on a non-stick baking sheet for 10–12 minutes until golden.

Serve warm.

Now, that Martini... Shaken or stirred?!

Makes

30 balls

Ingredients

30 pimento-stuffed green olives
150 g plain flour
100 g mature Cheddar cheese, grated
50 g vegetarian Italian hard cheese, grated
150 g unsalted butter
½ tsp smoked paprika
½ tsp cayenne pepper

SCOTCH QUAIL EGGS

Quail eggs make for a handy travel-sized version of this scrumptious classic snack.

Method

Add the white wine vinegar to a bowl containing 1 litre (2 pints) of very cold water, ready to cool the eggs.

Boil the quail eggs for 2 minutes and plunge into the cold water; leave to cool completely in the fridge. In a bowl mix the sausage meat, sage and seasoning.

Now the tricky bit: peeling the eggs! They're only soft boiled, so be gentle with them.

Create 12 round patties of sausage meat, roughly 6-cm (2½-in.) in diameter and place an egg in the centre of each, gently shaping the meat around the egg.

Roll each of the sausage meat balls in the flour followed by the beaten egg and lastly coat with the breadcrumbs. Leave to chill for at least 30 minutes before frying.

Half fill a deep saucepan with vegetable oil; heat to 190°C/375°F and fry the balls in small batches until golden.

Drain on kitchen paper. Best eaten warm but can be stored in the fridge and eaten cold for lunch the next day.

Makes

12 balls

Ingredients

2 tbsp white wine vinegar
12 quail eggs
500 g sausage meat
8 sage leaves, chopped
sea salt
ground black pepper
50 g plain flour
2 eggs, beaten
100 g fresh breadcrumbs
vegetable oil, for frying

FRENCH GOUGÈRES

These are the savoury version of profiteroles and are a delightful light cheesy ball: golden on the outside and fluffy on the inside.

Method

In a medium saucepan boil together the butter, salt and water.

Turn down the heat and add the flour while beating vigorously with a wooden spoon until the mixture comes away from the sides of the pan and forms a ball of dough.

Allow the dough to cool for a few minutes then start adding the beaten eggs a little at a time.

Keep beating until you've added all the egg then mix in the cheese.

Line a baking tray with non-stick parchment and place dessertspoonfuls of the mixture in rows, spaced out to allow for spreading.

Bake in a preheated oven at 200°C/400°F/Gas 6 for 20–25 minutes until puffed and golden.

Serve warm.

Makes

Approximately 24 balls

Ingredients

80 g unsalted butter
1 tsp sea salt
250 ml water
100 g plain flour
4 medium eggs, beaten
150 g Cheddar cheese

CRANBERRY AND GOAT CHEESE

These super-easy cheese balls add colour to your canapé platters. You can even eat the sticks!

Method

Place the goat cheese in a bowl and mash with the splash of olive oil until smooth.

Season with sea salt and pepper and roll the cheese into bite-sized balls, ready for coating.

Combine the coating ingredients and roll the balls in the mix to coat them.

Pop the balls on a tray and push half a pretzel stick into the centre of each one; cover and chill in the fridge.

These will keep in the fridge overnight.

Serve with your favourite dipping sauce.

Makes

Approximately 18 balls

Ingredients

For the cheese balls:
300 g rindless
    goat cheese
splash of extra-
    virgin olive oil
sea salt
cracked black pepper

For the coating:
2 tbsp parsley,
    finely chopped
2 tbsp dried cranberries,
    finely chopped
1 tbsp pistachios,
    finely chopped
½ tbsp chilli flakes
packet of 10
    pretzel sticks

JAPANESE RICE BALLS

These balls will add fun to mealtimes and lunch boxes. Get creative and experiment to find your favourite flavourings and coatings. You can even hide a surprise filling in the centre for extra flavour.

Method

Cook the sushi rice according to the packet's instructions and cool.

To make the balls, wet your hands and rub together with a pinch of salt. This stops the rice from sticking.

Take a bite-sized portion of rice – if you want to add a filling do it now by flattening the rice in your palm and adding a small amount of filling, then folding the rice around it and squeezing and rolling it into a ball.

Roll the balls in your chosen coatings or leave some naked if you prefer.

These are best eaten on the day they are made but will keep chilled in the fridge overnight.

Makes

Approximately 26 balls

Ingredients

For the rice balls:
175 g sushi rice
water
salt

Filling ideas:
miso paste and
    chopped nuts
pickled vegetables
    and ginger
nut butter or
    tahini paste

For the coating:
sesame seeds
chopped coriander
    and mint

BUTTERY POTATO DUMPLINGS

These gorgeous soft buttery dumpling delights are the epitome of comfort food. As they contain lots of butter, they should be enjoyed as a treat!

Method

To make the dough, combine the flour, polenta, salt, nutmeg and mashed potato with a wooden spoon.

Once mixed together make a well in the middle and add the beaten egg and melted butter. Mix again until the dough is smooth.

Boil a large pan of salted water while you form the dumpling balls. Roll bite-sized pieces of dough into balls. Flour your hands if the mix is a bit sticky.

Gently drop the dough balls into the boiling water, moving them around to stop them from sticking.

Once they float, they are ready. Drain and keep warm by covering with tin foil while you make the sauce.

For the sauce, chop and sauté the onions in butter and garlic powder until golden, and pour over the dumplings. Sprinkle with parsley and serve.

Makes

Approximately 10 balls

Ingredients

For the dumplings:
100 g plain flour, plus extra for rolling
30 g polenta
pinch of sea salt
pinch of grated nutmeg
300 g cooked mashed potatoes
1 medium egg, beaten
35 g salted butter, melted

For the sauce:
1 medium onion
125 g salted butter
1 tsp garlic powder
Handful of fresh parsley, finely chopped

Did you know?
Sev puri is a spicy, sweet and tangy Indian street snack.

SEV PURI PUFFS

Puris are deep-fried puffed dough balls traditionally filled with potatoes, onions, yoghurt and chutney, and topped with sev, a crunchy, flavoured noodle. Why not customise with your own fillings – there are no rules!

Method

To make the puris, mix the semolina, sea salt and enough water to knead into a soft dough.

Cover with a damp tea towel and leave to rest for 20 minutes.

Sprinkle a work surface with some fine semolina and roll out the dough until 2-cm (¾-in.) thick. Cut out 3-cm (1¼-in.) diameter rounds of dough using a pastry cutter.

Heat the vegetable oil in a pan and deep-fry in batches until very light brown and crisp. As they cook the dough will puff up into balls.

Leave to cool.

To fill the balls, make small holes in the tops of them and add your chosen fillings: a little bit of potato, onion, yoghurt, chutney, and finish with a sprinkle of sev and chopped coriander.

Makes

Approximately 18 balls

Ingredients

For the dough:
300 g very fine
    semolina, plus a
    little extra for rolling
sea salt
water
oil, to deep-fry

Filling suggestions:
cooked potato
onions, finely chopped
chutney — choose
    your favourites
sev
chopped coriander

CHEESY POTATO BALLS

Something magical happens when you cook cheese and potato in golden breadcrumbs.

Method

To the warm mashed potatoes add the butter, cheese, chives, seasoning, 1 egg and beat until smooth, then leave aside to cool.

Tip the potato mixture onto a floured surface, break off small pieces and roll into balls.

Dip each ball in the remaining beaten egg and then roll in the breadcrumbs, pressing lightly to get them to stick.

Place on a baking sheet and drizzle with some olive oil.

Bake in a preheated oven at 190°C/375°F/Gas 5 for about 20 minutes until golden.

Alternatively, you can shallow-fry these in vegetable oil if you prefer.

Eat them while they are hot... Delicious!

Makes

Approximately 24 balls

Ingredients

450 g potatoes, boiled
   and mashed
25 g salted butter
100 g grated hard
   cheese, such
   as Cheddar
1 tbsp fresh chives,
   chopped
sea salt
freshly ground
   black pepper
2 eggs
1 tbsp plain flour
60 g fresh breadcrumbs
olive oil, for drizzling
vegetable oil, for
   frying (optional)

MAC AND CHEESE BALLS

These cheesy balls will be loved by young and old alike and are guaranteed to become a party favourite.

Method

First make the macaroni cheese.

Boil the macaroni, following the packet's instructions, and drain thoroughly once cooked.

Make the cheese sauce by melting the butter in a saucepan and adding the flour, cooking the roux for a couple of minutes.

Add the milk and whisk constantly until it boils and thickens. Then add the cheese and seasonings. Stir in the macaroni and leave to cool.

Shape the cold mixture into balls (they may not be perfectly round but I'm sure you will be forgiven once people taste them) and roll them first into flour then the beaten egg and finally coat them with breadcrumbs. Heat the vegetable oil and shallow-fry in small batches, turning them until they are evenly golden.

Makes

Approximately 24 balls

Ingredients

For the filling:
225 g short-cut macaroni
65 g butter
75 g plain flour
900 ml whole milk
225 g grated
    Cheddar cheese
sea salt
freshly ground
    black pepper
½ tsp mustard or paprika

For the coating:
1 tbsp plain flour
1 egg, beaten
60–80 g fine dried
    breadcrumbs
vegetable oil, for frying

GARLIC DOUGH BALLS

These soft dough balls are the perfect excuse to indulge in lots of garlicky butter. They are so moreish that once you start, you'll find it hard to stop!

Method

Put the flour, yeast and olive oil into a bowl, add the salt and water, and mix with your hands to make a dough. Turn out the dough onto a floured surface and knead for 5–10 minutes until smooth. Pop the dough into an oiled bowl, cover with cling film and leave somewhere warm to double in size.

In the meantime, make the garlic butter: simply mix the butter and garlic together... and voila!

Back to the dough: knead the dough again for a few minutes and then divide it into approximately 30 sections, rolling them into small balls and placing them on a lightly oiled baking sheet – not too close together or they'll touch. Cover with cling film and leave them somewhere warm for another 30 minutes.

Remove the cling film and bake in a preheated oven at 200°C/400°F/Gas 6 for 16–18 minutes until they are risen and cooked through. Once they've cooled slightly it's time to dunk away in the garlicky butter!

Makes

Approximately 30 balls

Ingredients

For the dough balls:
325 g strong flour
7 g dried yeast
2 tbsp olive oil, plus extra for greasing
sea salt
250 ml lukewarm water
plain flour, for kneading

For the garlic butter:
100 g salted butter
2–3 cloves of garlic, crushed

CHEESE AND MUSHROOM ARANCINI

Fiddly but well worth the effort. You won't believe a fried rice ball can taste so good!

Method

Finely chop the onions and mushrooms. In a large saucepan gently sauté the onions in butter and oil until translucent.

Add the garlic and cook for another couple of minutes before adding the uncooked Arborio rice and mushrooms, mixing well.

Add the stock a ladle at a time, stirring until absorbed before adding another ladle. Keep going until the rice can't absorb any more, and remove from the heat.

Add the hard cheese and seasonings, allowing to cool slightly before stirring in the diced mozzarella. Pop in the fridge to chill for at least 30 minutes. Roll tablespoon-sized amounts into balls, before moving onto the coating.

First, coat the balls in the flour, then the beaten eggs and finally the breadcrumbs. Deep-fry for 4–5 minutes.

Delicious served as a starter with a spicy tomato dipping sauce. Alternatively, add a bed of crispy salad greens to create a wholesome main course.

Makes

Approximately 28 balls

Ingredients

For the balls:
2 onions
100 g mushrooms
25 g salted butter
2 tbsp olive oil
4 garlic cloves, crushed
300 g Arborio rice
1 litre vegetable stock
100 g vegetarian
    Italian hard cheese
sea salt
150 g mozzarella

For the coating:
60 g plain flour
2 eggs, beaten
120 g breadcrumbs
vegetable oil, for frying

OTHER AMAZE-BALLS
SWEET

Cake Pops • Cookie Dough Balls •
Plum Dumplings • Mini Jam Doughnuts •
Chocolate Truffles • Strawberry
Truffles • Profiteroles with Hot
Chocolate Sauce • Coconut Momos •
Unni Appam Banana Fritter

CAKE POPS

There'll be plenty of volunteers to help decorate these fun cake pops. You can make your own vanilla sponge, but a shop-bought sponge works just as well.

Method

First, make the buttercream. With a hand mixer or wooden spoon, beat the butter and icing sugar together until smooth before adding the vanilla and milk and beating again until smooth.

Add the crumbled cake into the buttercream and stir together. Using your hands roll a tablespoon of mixture into a ball and pop onto a baking tray.

Once you have a whole tray of cake balls push a lollipop stick into each one then put into the fridge to chill. Melt the chocolate in a bowl over a pan of hot water and dip each ball into it to coat it thoroughly with chocolate. Dip into the sprinkles and then stand them upright in a glass or pot until they set.

They will keep in a sealed container for 3–5 days. They don't need to go in the fridge, but don't leave them unattended as they will magically disappear!

Makes

Approximately 20 balls

Ingredients

For the cake pops:
75 g butter, softened
150 g icing sugar
½ tsp vanilla extract
1 tbsp milk
350 g vanilla sponge cake, crumbled

For the coating:
200 g dark chocolate
sprinkles, to dip
lolly sticks

COOKIE DOUGH BALLS

Everyone loves cookie dough, and making it into balls makes it even easier to eat. Too easy, perhaps...

Method

Soften the butter then beat it together with the sugar using a hand mixer or wooden spoon.

Next add the vanilla, flour and chocolate chips and mix again until thoroughly combined.

Finally add in the milk and keep mixing until you have a bowl full of delicious dough.

Start rolling it into balls. If you can manage not to eat it straight from the bowl, you should end up with about 12 yummy dough balls.

These will keep in a sealed container in the fridge for up to 5 days.

Makes

Approximately 12 balls

Ingredients

100 g salted butter
175 g soft brown sugar
2 tsp vanilla extract
140 g plain flour
2 tbsp chocolate chips
2 tbsp full-fat milk

PLUM DUMPLINGS

These European dumplings are a real comfort food. A ball of soft sweet potato wrapped around sweet juicy plums!

Experiment with different coatings – cinnamon or sugar would work nicely. If plums aren't in season you could substitute them with dried plums or even plum jam.

Method

In a mixing bowl combine the cooled riced potatoes, flour, semolina, butter, sugar, egg yolk and salt and work quickly to make a smooth dough.

Cover the bowl with a clean tea towel and leave in a cool place for the dough to rest for 15–30 minutes.

Pop a sugar cube inside each of the pitted plums.

Divide the dough into 12 portions and wrap them around each plum until it's fully tucked up inside with no gaps!

Cook the dumplings in simmering water for about 12 minutes until they float to the surface.

Remove with a slotted spoon and roll in the poppy seeds.

Eat while they are warm: they're wonderful with thick whipped cream!

Makes

Approximately 12 balls

Ingredients

For the dumplings:
400 g starchy potatoes, cooked and riced
100 g whole wheat flour
30 g semolina
30 g unsalted butter, softened
25 g caster sugar
1 egg yolk
pinch of sea salt
12 ripe plums, washed and pitted
12 sugar cubes

For the coating:
60 g poppy seeds

MINI JAM DOUGHNUTS

How amazing to have mini warm doughnuts, coated in sugar with jam oozing out... You'll be popular when you make these!

Method

Mix the yeast with half a teaspoon of sugar and 2 tablespoons of milk; leave in a warm place for 15 minutes.

Put the flour, salt and a teaspoon of sugar in a bowl. Make a well in the centre and add the yeast mixture, melted butter, remaining milk and egg.

Mix well, then knead for a few minutes. Cover the bowl with a clean tea towel before setting aside until the dough doubles in size.

Tip the dough onto a floured surface, knead again for a few minutes, then divide into 24 balls. Leave in a warm place again until the balls double in size.

Heat the oil in a deep sided saucepan to 190°C/375°F then fry 2–3 balls at a time for 3–5 minutes until they are golden, turning with a metal slotted spoon halfway through. Drain on kitchen paper then coat with the remaining sugar.

To add the filling, slit the tops with a sharp knife and pierce into the middles with a skewer then pipe in a little jam.

Makes

Approximately 24 balls

Ingredients

For the dough:
1 tbsp dried yeast
4 tbsp caster sugar
150 ml milk, warmed
225 g plain flour, sieved, plus extra for kneading
¼ tsp sea salt
50 g butter, melted
1 egg, beaten
350 ml vegetable oil, for frying

For the filling:
approximately 4 tbsp smooth raspberry jam

CHOCOLATE TRUFFLES

You'll need to prepare these truffles a day ahead, but they are truly worth it. Perfect as a gorgeous home-made gift or a decadent end to a dinner party.

Method

Pop the cream, butter and brandy in a small saucepan and slowly bring to a simmer.

Blitz the chocolate in a food processor and, while still running, slowly pour the cream mixture onto the chocolate, blending it until the mixture is smooth. Add Greek yoghurt and blend briefly to combine.

Transfer to a clean bowl and cover with cling film; it will be quite runny and will need to set in the fridge overnight.

For the coating, put the chocolate and oil in a bowl and melt over a pan of hot water.

Remove the truffle mixture from the fridge and dust your hands with raw cacao powder. Take teaspoons of the mixture and roll them into balls.

Using cocktail sticks or skewers, dip the balls into melted chocolate until completely covered, then pop them onto non-stick parchment, sprinkle with chocolate shavings and leave to set. These will last for at least 7 days in the fridge.

Makes

Approximately 30 balls

Ingredients

For the truffles:
150 ml thick
    double cream
25 g unsalted butter
2 tbsp brandy
150 g dark chocolate
    (70–75 per
    cent cocoa)
1 tbsp Greek yoghurt

For the coating:
225 g dark chocolate
1 tsp groundnut oil
raw cacao powder,
    for rolling
chocolate shavings
    – your choice

STRAWBERRY TRUFFLES

It's a match made in heaven – deliciously rich chocolate blending beautifully with the intense fruity flavour of strawberries.

Method

Pop the cream, butter and liqueur in a small saucepan and slowly bring to a simmer.

Blitz the chocolate in a food processor and, with it still running, slowly pour the cream mixture onto the chocolate and keep blending until the mixture is smooth.

Add the Greek yoghurt and blend briefly to combine.

Transfer to a clean bowl and cover with cling film; it will be quite runny and will need to set in the fridge overnight.

Remove the truffle mixture from the fridge and dust your hands with cacao powder. Then take teaspoons of the mixture and roll them into balls before coating them with the freeze-dried strawberries.

These will last for at least 7 days in the fridge.

Makes

Approximately 30 balls

Ingredients

For the truffles:
150 ml thick
    double cream
25 g unsalted butter
2 tbsp strawberry
    liqueur (or syrup
    for an alcohol-
    free variation)
150 g dark chocolate
    (70–75 per
    cent cocoa)
1 tbsp Greek yoghurt

For the coating:
raw cacao powder
freeze-dried
    strawberry pieces

PROFITEROLES WITH HOT CHOCOLATE SAUCE

Light crisp pastry shells filled with cream and topped off with a silky rich chocolate sauce – irresistible!

Method

Preheat the oven to 200°C/400°F/Gas 6. Add the butter and water to a saucepan and bring to the boil until the butter has melted.

Add the flour and sugar, and beat with a hand mixer or wooden spoon for 1–2 minutes until it forms a smooth ball of dough. Add the eggs, a little at a time, and keep mixing after each addition until you have a smooth glossy paste.

Put teaspoons of the cooled mixture 2.5-cm (1-in.) apart on a non-stick baking sheet and bake for 25–30 minutes until golden.

Pierce the side of each to let out the steam and place back in the oven for another couple of minutes. Set aside to cool on a wire rack. Once completely cold slit them and fill with whipped cream.

When ready to serve, prepare the sauce: melt the chocolate with the water in a bain-marie, stirring gently. Drizzle over the profiteroles and enjoy!

Makes

Approximately 30 balls

Ingredients

For the pastry:
50 g salted butter
150 ml water
60 g strong flour, sieved
1 tsp caster sugar
2 large eggs, beaten

For the filling:
275 ml double cream, whipped

For the chocolate sauce:
175 g dark chocolate (70–75 per cent cocoa)
120 ml water

Did you know?
If you don't have a steamer, you can make your own with a lidded saucepan, four satsuma-sized balls of aluminium foil to form a makeshift trivet, and an ovenproof plate that's slightly smaller than the saucepan. Pop the foil balls in the saucepan and add 3-cm (1¼-in.) depth of water. Place the plate with the dumplings on into the saucepan, letting it rest on the foil balls. Replace the saucepan lid and turn on the heat to start steaming.

COCONUT MOMOS

A simplified version of traditional Tibetan steamed dumplings. Usually filled with veggies or meat, here they're yummy balls of sweetness!

Method

For the dough, combine the flour, oil and salt together, and slowly mix in the water. Knead until soft and non-sticky. Cover with a clean tea towel and keep aside for at least 30 minutes.

While the dough rests, mix all the filling ingredients together and put to one side.

Roll the dough on a floured surface and use an 8-cm (3¼-in.) cutter to make small circles.

Place a teaspoon of filling in the middle of each circle and carefully bring the dough together by folding and pinching the top, then roll in your palm to create a ball.

Lay the momos so they aren't touching in a greased steamer on a sheet of baking parchment (pierce some holes in the parchment to let the steam through). You may need to do this in 3 batches.

Steam for at least 10 minutes until they look transparent and don't feel sticky. Serve hot!

Makes

Approximately 15 balls

Ingredients

For the dough:
150 g plain flour
— plus extra
for dusting
5 tsp sunflower oil
pinch of sea salt
60 ml lukewarm water

For the filling:
75 g shredded coconut
25 g raisins
50 g brown sugar
¼ tsp ground
cinnamon
¼ tsp ground nutmeg
¼ tsp ground
cardamom

Did you know?
Jaggery is a completely unrefined sugar made from sugar cane juice that is reduced and set into blocks. It has a flavour somewhere between molasses and caramel.

UNNI APPAM
BANANA FRITTER

Unni Appam is a traditional Keralan snack; think of 'spiced-up' banana fritters and you're close. You'll need a mini ball cake pan for this recipe.

Method

Gently toast the coconut in half a teaspoon of oil until golden; leave to cool. Heat the jaggery in a small pan with water until melted; sieve and leave to cool. Dry toast the flours for about a minute. Mash the banana until smooth.

Mix the coconut, jaggery, banana and flours, adding enough water to create a smooth batter of dropping consistency. Leave for 15 minutes at room temperature, covered with a clean tea towel, and then add the remaining ingredients and mix to combine.

Preheat the oven to 200°C/400°F/Gas 6, pop a teaspoon of oil in each hole of the mini ball cake pan and heat for 3–5 minutes.

Add 1 tablespoon of the mixture to each hole and cook until air bubbles form on the surface; flip them over and cook the other side. They're ready when a cocktail stick comes out cleanly with no raw batter.

Makes

Approximately 18 balls

Ingredients

50 g fresh coconut, finely chopped
120 ml jaggery or 120 g muscovado sugar
60 ml water
115 g rice flour
35 g whole wheat flour
1 ripe banana
pinch of sea salt
pinch of baking powder
½ tsp cardamom powder
1 tsp roasted sesame seeds
oil, for frying

IMAGE CREDITS

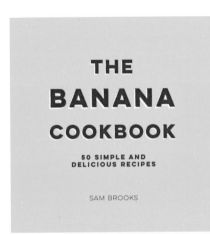

THE BANANA COOKBOOK

50 SIMPLE AND DELICIOUS RECIPES

Sam Brooks

£8.99
Hardback
ISBN: 978-1-78685-983-9

VEGAN SNACKS

SIMPLE, DELICIOUS SWEET AND SAVOURY TREATS

Elanor Clarke

£8.99
Hardback
ISBN: 978-1-78685-970-9

If you're interested in finding out more about our books,
find us on Facebook at *Summersdale Publishers*
and follow us on Twitter at *@summersdale*.

www.summersdale.com